A Passion-Filled Life

**37 daily devotional messages
to inspire the Christian believer
into a deeper faith**

Dedication

Like my other books, this is dedicated to my two precious
daughters,

Sarah and Heather.

Your love will always be my very heartbeat. I love you
both so very much!

Also, I dedicate this book to my grandson,

Blain Aaron.

What a joy you are in my life! I will always pray for God's
blessings in your life.

And finally, I dedicate this book to my parents,

John and Dorlene

I love you, Mom and Dad!

Table of Contents

A Challenging Purpose

Reference Scripture: Colossians 2:1-10

I am taken aback by the demeanor of Paul in the second chapter of Colossians. Without even a hint of a 'Hey, look at me and what I'm doing' attitude, he told this young church that he had a very specific purpose in mind and was laboring to complete the task—for their sake.

Why is that impressive to me? The reason is that he had not yet personally met these individuals. Still, he was laboring, struggling, and facing many difficulties in foreign lands for their sake. He continually prayed for, encouraged, and supported them. I have a hard time understanding why would he do that. Don't you?

After all, this is a world of selfish sentiments like 'look out for #1' and 'God helps those who help themselves'. Those and other sentiments have become the prevailing attitudes of most modern people. But, when we enter into Christ's family, we are to begin seeing people and things the way He wants us to. That means that we are to love others as He loved them and consider them above ourselves. It also means we should joyfully offer aid, comfort, encouragement, support, exhortation, or whatever else is needed by our brothers and sisters, that they might 'have the full riches of complete understanding' of God!

Paul's attitude here makes me question my own. So let me ask all of us the questions I am asking myself. Do we want to understand the complete treasures of wisdom and knowledge in Christ? Do we honestly want to be known as His children? If so, then just as we at one time asked Jesus to become the Lord of our lives, we must continue to live in Him, rooted and built up in Him, true to and strengthened in the faith, and overflowing in thankfulness. To continue to live in Him means to let Him be the guide and motivator of our lives, letting His cause become our purpose in life. Being rooted and built up in Him, as well as being true to and strengthened in the faith, means to be grounded in His teachings and be firm in our convictions. It also means to produce genuine, right and proper actions that are prompted by our faith. To overflow with thankfulness means to be always mindful that the Almighty God came to earth as a man of flesh and bone to willingly offer Himself as a sacrifice that opened up this relationship between Himself and us. He paid a king's ransom for our souls—the king's life for the pauper—not to take our lives away in slavery, but to offer us a new life of freedom, joy and peace! For that, how could we not be thankful?

Would we desire all of this for ourselves? Would our purpose today be to encourage others in God's love that they might receive the full riches of Christ? Oh, what a world we would have if we all would! If only we would! That was Paul's desire, prayer, plan and purpose. Dare we make it ours today?

Have a wonderful day in His grace!

An Awe-inspired People

Reference Scripture: Deuteronomy 5:23-29

What a picture this presents to the reader! Here was Moses, after receiving the 10 Commandments, delivering them to an awestruck people. And why were they awe-struck? It was because they had previously believed that anyone who saw the LORD, Jehovah, God, or even heard His voice would surely die because of their utter worthlessness to Him. And they were right! Sin could not enter into God's presence. It never was able back then, cannot now, and never will in the future. Only those sinful humans who are justified—made right, or righteous—by faith in God's grace are able to enter into His presence. That's part of the Gospel message, is it not?

But, there was Moses! He came down the mountain, still very much alive, after spending an extended period of time with God. He had been speaking with God had given him the Commandments. He was very much alive. Even more, his face radiated God's glory!

But then, fear set in... maybe only Moses could! After all, Moses was the chosen deliverer and leader of the people. They must have thought, "Maybe he would not be killed for being in God's presence, but surely we would." From our perspective, it seems silly, doesn't it? Surely, if they were going to die, they would have already done so! They were silly, weren't they?

Hmm... Maybe. But, at least they had a healthy respect for the Almighty Creator God, Jehovah. They revered His power and might. They worshipped His majesty. They honored His sovereignty. They stood—rather they fell down on their faces—in the deepest of sincere submission to this holy God. Oh, what a lesson we should find here. And do you see the result? God praised their response! He even gave them a great compliment! He said that what these people had said was good, and for it they and their children would be blessed forever if they would continue to respect and honor Him!

Would we respect our Lord is such a way? Would we break out of our modern thought that God is watching from a distance and understand that He's near enough to be involved? Would we rethink our supposition that we are self-made people and recognize instead that we are God's workmanship? Would we take another look at our self-gratifying boast of self-sufficiency and understand that we are to submit to His loving provision? Would we dare admit our fears, failings, weaknesses, double-minded-ness, sins and inadequacies?   Hopefully we will. Everything we need for life and godliness has already been given to us by God. Everything we have...including the breath we just took...is either on loan to us or is a gift of God's grace. So, wouldn't it be wise to have a healthy respect and awe for the One who holds our lives in the palm of His hand, grants us His grace and offers us His great and precious gifts?

Oh that our hearts would be so inclined to fear the Lord... Oh that mine would…

Have a wonderful day in His grace!

Because of Our Hope in Christ

Reference Scripture: Colossians 1:2-8

A prayer of thanksgiving was offered by the great missionary, Paul, to the Church at Colossae. From his opening words, "Grace and peace to you" through the whole letter he offered great blessings, thanksgiving, and concern. You see, he cared about them. He wished them the best offerings he could, that they receive the great and wonderful personal touches from God and that God would express His great love for them. What greater offering can we give someone than to offer this heartfelt blessing for the Lord of Heaven and Earth to touch them in His infinite love and tender mercy?

Then Paul went on to express why he would write this blessing to them. They had touched his heart and encouraged him in his missionary work by being faithful to the calling of Christ. He knew that they were living out their faith and had love for the body of Christ, the church. He knew that they had been touched by the Gospel of Christ because he heard news about these believers in Colossae. They lifted his spirit as he sat in prison. They encouraged his heart that his labor and afflictions were not in vain. So he prayed for great blessings to come upon them. They encouraged him to believe that his work wasn't yet done and that he must continue to pour out his heart to people everywhere to point them to Christ Jesus, our Lord.

It must have been their sincerity that moved Paul so greatly. He noted that their faith and love came from the hope of their future reward with Christ. Their hope motivated their actions. They hadn't simply received a personal hope and said, "Great, I'm saved," only to go on living as they had been. They hadn't simply received God's grace and hoarded it for themselves. They hadn't even received it and only shared it with a few others that surrounded them, neglecting others that they might have deemed unlovable. No, they received the gift of God's grace and love, the gift of salvation in Christ, and then, overflowing in their joy, they offered it out for all to receive. Their hope in Christ was so great that they indiscriminately and unreservedly offered it to others. That moved Paul to write to them and tell them how much he was encouraged to rejoice in his own sufferings for their sake (see Col 1:24).

May the Spirit of God move in our hearts today to enact the love of God by living it out for others to see. May He move us so that we might offer it for others to receive. May we encourage others along our paths to accept the love of God for themselves. May we all be faithful ministers of Christ on someone else's behalf!

And may we all have a wonderful day in His grace!

Concern for the Body of Christ

Reference Scripture: Colossians 1:2-14

The beginning of the letter from Paul to the Colossian church is filled with a deeply personal message. Paul wanted this church to know how much he cared for them and how much he desired that they please God in their lives.

Are we that interested in the lives of those around us? Do we honestly desire the best of God's blessings in their lives? When they come to Christ, do we encourage them to grow deeper in the knowledge of God's will and that they gain spiritual wisdom and understanding? Or do we tell them that it is a great thing that they have done and then simply begin talking about the latest football game or television show?

I believe that one of the greatest differences between Paul and us is that he cared about new believers in Christ enough to give his life in service to building them up in the body of Christ. He gave all of his time and effort in teaching them and encouraging them to grow to maturity in their faith, to please God in their lifestyles, and to continue spreading the Gospel of Christ. He didn't take a superficial view of his spiritual condition and say, "I'm saved, so I'm okay." No, while he continued instructing and encouraging others he considered himself still in training so that, as he said, "after I have preached to others, I myself will not be disqualified for the prize." (See 1 Corinthians 9:27 NIV) Paul lived his life in service to Christ by living in service to Christ's body—the church—which is the group of believers worldwide. His reason, of course, was so that everyone he met could be presented to God as a believer in Christ.

Why, then, since so much of Paul's teaching fills the New Testament, is modern Christianity considered to be simple church attendance? Why is Christianity more of a social gathering than spiritual one? Why is the body of Christ fractured through the isolations that we call denominations? Jesus' own prayer was that His disciples and all of those who would believe would be one even as the Father and He were one (John 17:21). Why, then, are we, as Christ's body, missing the goal of unity in the faith that Christ Himself gave us? Perhaps the reason is that we have failed to understand these things Paul gave up his lie to teach.

Let us never stop asking God to fill believers with knowledge, wisdom and understanding that they live lives worthy of the Lord and please Him in every way. Someday, we who are more mature now might need to rely on the prayers of those who are only babes in Christ today to get us through our difficult times. If we don't encourage them today, so that they might grow to maturity, and if we do not work toward unity in the faith today, they may not be there for us on that day when we need their prayers and encouragement. What a shame that will be...

Pray for believers today, in honesty and sincerity, that they might truly understand the depths of God's love and understand His will in their lives. Pray for yourself that you might as well. And have a wonderful day in His grace!

Defeat Discouragement!

Reference Scripture: Romans 8:26-39

More than conquerors! Is that what we feel like? The Greek word translated as more than is a prefix 'huper' (hoop-er'). From this we get our prefix 'hyper', meaning 'extra' or 'super'. So do we feel like "super" conquerors over the stresses and tribulations of our daily lives? Do we feel like we have a handle on our lives? Do we rise above the mess of selfish humanity that we live in, or do we fail to realize our "super" conqueror position in life?

Is this all because we are just better than everyone else? Are we stronger, more able, and more...whatever...than everyone else? Absolutely not! But, the Spirit of Christ is! Christ Jesus, Himself is! Our great God in Heaven is! And if they—all ONE and yet all Three—are on our side, who could ever stand against us? What trial could hold or souls or our hearts hostage? Our Lord is on our side. Think about that!

- Jesus lived, died, and resurrected, so nothing in this life can touch Him—or us if we live in Him!
- Jesus was before all things, in Him all things were created, and He declared Himself to be eternal. So no thing that exists or is bound by time can hurt us or hinder us.
- Jesus defeated Satan's stronghold of sin over humanity, so no demon, angel, spiritual entity or ruler could harm us!
- Jesus calmed the storms, the wind, the waves, He healed the lame, the blind, the deaf, and He raised the dead. Now, nothing that has dimension, takes up space, or is of this world can steal God's love from us!

All that boils down to this, if Christ is for us, how are we not like super conquerors? Who can stand against Him? All of the power of the God-head is in Him and He promised in John 14 to be in us if we obey Him and that He and the Father will make Their home with us if we love Him. Therefore, yes we can—and have—overcome! But we did not do this through ourselves. We have overcome through HIM!

Do you feel like a weary soldier? Do you see yourself as a wounded conqueror? Then take heart, your savior helps you in your time of weakness, because when you are weak He is ultimately strong!

Have a wonderful day in His grace!

Deliberate In Prayer

Reference Scripture: 1 Timothy 1:18-2:8

It seems that Paul was very concerned with the prayer life of believers. He felt it important in his own life and it seems practiced it very often. He also urged all believers he met to do the same. Further, he exhorted that they should be 'devoted' to prayer (Col 4:2) and faithful to prayer (Romans 12:12).

But, the teaching didn't begin with Paul. Through the ages men have prayed to gods. Often it was to plead for mercy from the elements or from something else that had caused fear in their hearts. Too often, however, their prayers were directed to lifeless idols that were incapable of offering any true assistance. Yet, to the believer in a living and All-Powerful God, prayer is a two-way communication. Well, at least it should be. The problem is that in our modern lives we fail to make sure time for prayer is put onto our schedule or in our day-timers and Blackberries. We simply do not place a priority on it. And even if we do, distractions interrupt or stresses of the day block our concentration so that the communication never happens. We hope that saying grace at dinner time will count for something on our prayer report card.

Whatever the reason—whatever the excuse (I've used them, too)—prayer simply cannot be ignored or mis-prioritized. Would my children know I love them if I fail to tell them? Would my parents? The simple fact is that when we care for someone we communicate with them or they may never know that we care. And the same goes for our loving Heavenly Father.

So, what is one to do? How about this: Plan to pray. Really. Plan it. Plan the 'when' to pray (both the time when to start and a time to end if necessary). Put it into the day's schedule. Plan the 'where' to pray (a regular prayer place. Remember, Jesus even mentioned a prayer closet). Plan the 'what' to pray (otherwise known as a prayer list). And lastly, plan an accountability for your prayer time. Ok, so the concept isn't really new with me, and it seems clumsy to have to plan it all. But if it enables us to become disciplined in our communications with God it is a great idea to start with, right? Cut out all of the excuses by planning it all beforehand. After all, if prayer were an important television show we wanted to watch we would plan to watch it. If it were that sporting event we anticipated we would plan our schedule so that we would not miss it. If it were that great restaurant we wanted to try we would make sure we tried it. Right? Seriously, if communication with our God was as important as these things, we'd make certain arrangements to pray. I'm sure God would want to talk about whatever subject is on your mind, even if you have to make Him an appointment to discuss just that one topic. He'd probably rather discuss just one topic than none at all.

Besides, in these days of turmoil and rampant mental diseases that cause people to do incredibly horrible things to others, why would it seem to be inconvenient to schedule a specific time with the lover of or souls and the giver of solace, comfort and peace?

Those are just a few thoughts for the morning. Perhaps now would be a good time for a prayer? Go on...your Father wants to talk with you.

Have a wonderful day in His grace!

Delighting in Weakness

Reference Scripture: 2 Corinthians 12:7-10

I've often pondered what this passage was all about. I've heard many people explain what they thought Paul's thorn in the flesh was. I, too, have my own thoughts, but what it was really doesn't matter. His point was that it proved his human weakness and showed Christ's strength and greatness. It brought a continual reminder that when Paul was weak, Christ remained strong and offered that strength to Paul.

I'm reminded of my life in all of this. I have difficulties in my business. I have difficulties at home. I have weaknesses in my character. I have burdens on my heart. I have ailments in my body. I have frustrations in my mind. I have stresses in my life. Does this sound familiar to you? Sure it does. We *all* have these! These are just *some* of our human weaknesses. The great thing, though, is that Christ has none of these in Himself, and so He offers us all of His grace and strength to bring us through all of these things!

Furthermore, I'm reminded of an expression that makes great sense. It's a simple though: Stressed is simply desserts spelled backwards! Are you stressed and anxious, worried and burdened? If so, then turn around from those burdens and look to Christ! He has the sweetness to make all of life's trials sweeter and easier to bear! He has the answer to your difficulties and He is the bread of life, a fount of living water, and your dessert for this lifetime. If we are faithful to complete this troublesome earthly life as a believer in Christ, He will offer that dessert we call heaven. What a wonderful thought!

This all reminds me of the funeral for my aunt many years back. Though obviously a time of mourning for the family left behind, it was also a time of celebration for her life which she lived to honor her Lord as she served others in His love. I was reminded that stressed is desserts spelled backwards when I listened to my aunt's pastor speak about her life. It seemed that whenever she offered something to eat to someone at her house, or when there was a church dinner, as she picked up someone's plate, she told the person to keep his fork because "the best was yet to come." Of course, she meant the dessert that was yet to come. The wonderful thing about this was that this was the way she lived her life. Her body was worn from over 80 years of life and a 20+ year battle with cancer, but she lived her life in just the same way as that church dinner...the best was yet to come. Friends—and family—the best is now here for her! All of her pains and trials and stresses are gone, her dessert has arrived! Ours will someday, too!

May that be the theme of our lives, that the best is yet to come, when our sorrows will turn to joy, our weaknesses will be girded with the strength of the Lord, and our stresses be turned into desserts!

Have a wonderful day in His grace!

Distinct and Lavished

Reference Scripture: Ephesians 1:3-12

What a beautiful thing to consider...a distinct spiritual blessing that God lavished all of that grace on us with all wisdom and understanding. Some translations will use the word 'in' instead of 'with'. This is because the preposition 'en' in Greek can be translated either way. As a result, both translations are acceptable. Even better, both hold a blessing for us this very day!

If the word 'with' is used it represents an additional blessing on top of the grace given. Wisdom and understanding are offered and essential so that we can fathom what God has done for us through Christ. As Paul said to the Corinthian church, God, in His wisdom, understood that "the world through its wisdom did not know him," so "God was pleased through the foolishness of what was preached to save those who believe," and that the message preached was "Christ crucified: a stumbling block to Jews and foolishness to Gentiles...[for] to those whom God has called, both Jews and Greeks, Christ the power of God and the wisdom of God...the foolishness of God is wiser than man's wisdom, and the weakness of God is stronger than man's strength" (see 1 Corinthians 1:21-25 NIV). So, with all of that said, God has granted us special wisdom that the world around us does not realize. It is because of the wisdom that comes through Christ that we can understand the significance of all of His work on our behalf. The spiritual fulfillment of Jesus' words, "he who has ears, let him hear" is this, "he who has received grace, let him understand."

Still, if we consider the translation more understandable using the word 'in' instead of 'with', it simply puts the emphasis on the depth of the wisdom and understanding of God. We are told in Isaiah 28:29 that the LORD Almighty's "plan is wonderful" and His "wisdom is magnificent." And we are told that it was "by wisdom the LORD laid the earth's foundations, by understanding he set the heavens in place" (Proverbs 3:19). None of us can fathom the depths of what God knows about the history of creation, the secrets of men's hearts, the details of mankind's future, or what eternity will really be like. Yet, in His infinite wisdom and understanding, He offered us the grace of His presence and His love, lavishing it on us like a spring shower drenches the tender grass and budding flowers.

Whichever thought you subscribe to, both are entirely accurate and full of a rich bounty of encouragement for you today. The trials you face do not demand that your heart remain heavy. The grace of the LORD Almighty has been poured out on you that through it all you might recognize that His grace is a great power. It is truly and absolutely sufficient to see you through any trial you face today or that lays ahead of you. No grace is greater to calm fears and lift burdens, to heal the soul and mend the broken heart. No grace, but the grace of the Wonderful Counselor, Mighty God, Prince of Peace can save and preserve you. Rest in Him today!

And with that, have a wonderful day in His grace!

Dwelling on Inspiration

Reference Scripture: 1 Corinthians 2:9-14

There is an interesting thought pattern found here in this passage. It is one that believers in Christ ought to dwell on often, for it might allow a greater faith to grow within our hearts if we follow the whole thought.

First, we find that no man can truly fathom what God really has planned for His people. Even the apostle John, in his glimpse into heaven that we read about in the Revelation, could not describe the wondrous appearance of heaven in anything but the most exquisite lustrous metals and jewels of his time. It is obvious, though, that the appearance was so much more glorious than even these precious things could express. No eye has ever really seen what God has prepared for us.

Second, no ear has heard the voice of God expressing the fathomless depths of His love for all people. We read of His love in His marvelous love letter we call the Bible. We begin to comprehend His love as we meditate upon the actions of His Son, Jesus of Nazareth, the Christ, our Savior. We accept in faith that the miraculous working of His grace on our behalf is the expression of His love toward us. We rely and hope on that love as being eternal as we read that it is in the Scripture. But, who has ever truly grasped how wide, how long, how deep His love truly is?

And finally, whose heart has truly understood all of the riches of understanding regarding the whys, and wherefores that God would consider us for even just one moment? God, the Almighty—Creator of the universe and all life—the Author and Creator of our faith—Sustainer of life—is infinitely pure and ultimately holy. Why then would He bother with mere mortal, sinful, selfish beings like us? What does He really want from us? Whose heart can fully know all of the riches and treasures of complete understanding our faithful and loving Lord?

Yet, God truly does love us! We are His creation. He honestly desires our fellowship. He deeply treasures the communion of the created with the Creator. He cherishes the energy, time, money and talents we offer to Him as our token responses to His unending love. He truly desires for us to be united with Him in mind, body and spirit and for us to worship Him in spirit and in truth. And if these things are what He truly desires, should they not inspire us to desire the same with Him? Sure they should! The only question is...do they?

Have a wonderful day in His grace!

Excuses or Sincerity

Reference Scripture: Galatians 6:1-10

Through the years, I've heard believers use a very interesting justification for them to continue to practicing their sinful actions. Often I've heard them say, "Oh, it's just my nature. That's the way I was made." It's as if temptation was made just for them and vice versa. That justification leads to a conclusion that, "God knows who I am, so I'm ok. He understands..." Well, it is true that God knows who each one of us is. He knows our human tendency to sin. And yes, He understands it. But, that does not mean that He approves of it!

You see, God made man in His image. Adam was made to fellowship with a holy God in a perfect world but chose instead to follow a different path and sinned against God. Scripture tells us that his action of disobedience is the reason why we have a sinful nature at work in our bodies. His sin—being the father of the human race—is the origin of our sin, and no human as a result is clean and holy before God on his own merit, choice, or work. Man must have a new nature to walk in relationship with an eternal, holy God. Man must have a rebirth of spirit. He must be born again or sin will reign forever in his life...and death. That's the beginning of the Gospel message which we know goes on to tell us of the Christ, Jesus of Nazareth, who was God in the flesh, crucified, died, buried, and rose again to pay the penalty of our sin and to offer us that new life in the Spirit of God. It was His actions on our behalf that completely—not just partially—nullifies any justification for continuing the practice of sin mentioned above. His action on our behalf restores those who believe on Him to a new nature, holy and acceptable to God.

You see, Paul told us that if any man is in Christ, he is a new creation. The old is dead and gone! The old man is dead and buried in Christ's tomb. We are dead to sin, but alive to God in Christ! The sinful nature was crucified with Christ! We are no longer slaves to sinfulness. How could a believer in Christ—repentant, forgiven, and baptized into a new life in Christ—continue to live in something that no longer exists for them? We cannot continue to practice our sinful ways, boldly excusing ourselves on the basis of our old sinful nature, and expect God to offer us His grace. Paul said that would be "mocking" God and that continuing to do this will bring about destruction and ruin. On the contrary, we must sow to please the new nature, the Spirit of God. From this will come a wonderful reward.

May we never be ones to claim that our old nature caused us to sin. No, instead let us approach our God in truthfulness and rely upon His grace when we sin, humbly coming before Him to ask His forgiveness for our decision to turn our backs on the new creation He has made within us. May we never bring excuses to Him. That would only prove our insincerity which is something that will never please God.

Have a wonderful day in His grace!

Finding the Ancient Faith

Reference Scripture: Psalm 17

I have always enjoyed reading this psalm. It is the humble prayer of one whose heart yearned to be what God required. Though it was a bold move to invite the Almighty to examine him, David knew that his heart and mind were set on God's goals. Then on top of that, he resolved—firmly decided in advance—that he would not let his mouth utter sinful words, for he knew what Jesus would later teach: "The good man brings good things out of the good stored up in his heart, and the evil man brings evil things out of the evil stored up in his heart. For out of the overflow of his heart his mouth speaks" (Luke 6:45 NIV).

Still, David knew that God listens to the prayers of His children, so he prayed. In tough times he prayed. In good times he prayed. When he was hungry, he prayed. When he was in danger he prayed. When he was satisfied he praised (which is really a prayer of thanksgiving). And when he was delivered, he praised. This constant communication with Jehovah was the strength of his faith.

Why, then, does it seem so tough for us modern people to be that resolved and devoted? Why does it seem so tough to focus our lives on the task of living to glorify God? Maybe David had the key. He prayed. He stayed in contact with Almighty God on a regular basis. Furthermore, He sought to please God in his living by resolving to do so. Maybe modern faith is like the thousands of self-help books that you can find on bookshelves across America today. They might all have some amount of worth in some fashion or other, but unless the reader is 'resolved' to put what he reads into practice, every last one of those books is really worthless. So it is with our faith. If we are not resolved to put it into practice, it really is worthless to help us.

So let's grab hold of the ancient faith...one that lives and breathes in the will of God. Let's seek the kingdom of God and His righteousness first and foremost in our lives, and see what will accomplish in our lives then! Then, when we doubt as to whether or not our modern faith is all it should be, "This is what the LORD says: 'Stand at the crossroads and look; ask for the ancient paths, ask where the good way is, and walk in it, and you will find rest for your souls'" (Jeremiah 6:16 NIV).

Have a wonderful day in Him!

Fleeing and Pursuing

Reference Scripture: 2 Timothy 2:22-26

In the midst of instructing Timothy on how to lead a church and how to live appropriately in response to the Gospel of Christ, Paul enters this passage into the mix. One has to bring to mind the words of James when this passage is read. James asked, "What causes fights and quarrels among you? Don't they come from your desires that battle within you? You want something but don't get it. You kill and covet, but you cannot have what you want" (James 4:1-2 NIV). Therefore, James said, "You quarrel and fight." Note that Paul seems to equate quarreling with the evil desires of youth. By fleeing these desires, one can turn to pursue the opposite of the selfish ambition and vain conceits that cause quarreling. The opposite of these self-centered, self-gratifying (and therefore, sinful) things is righteousness, faith, love, and peace.

Isn't that an elemental teaching of Christianity? Sure it is. We are to forsake our sinful nature—crucify it with Christ—in order to take on a Godly and mature nature, created to be like God in true righteousness and holiness (Ephesians 4:22-24). We are to put off deceit, falsehoods, bitterness, rage, anger, brawling, slander and every other form of malice. Instead, we are to be kind and compassionate with one another, and forgive each other (Ephesians 4:29-32). Oh, but that's so tough to do. Isn't it? Sure it is! That's why it takes the "new self" that Paul talked about in Ephesians. Our old self is full of every-thing that is selfish and unyielding to anything that is not in line with its interests and beliefs. We will fight and argue over anything while we live in our old nature. But our new nature has been created to be like Christ who, even when being brutally beaten and murdered, He would not utter anything but love and forgiveness from his mouth. Our new nature has been created to be like His, which was full of compassion. Our new self has been created to be a God-honoring, God-pleasing nature, not a combative and self-centered, argumentative one.

So, instead, we are to be gentle and compassionate to those who would disagree with us. We are to hope that, through our gentleness, the Spirit of God will convict hearts and draw unbelievers to Christ. We are to teach in kindness and sensitivity, but in sincerity and with the authority of the Word of God. Through it all, we should never quarrel. After all, if we're full of quarreling and abuse, who would want to come to Christ and be around us? But if we live in a Godly way, then the teaching about God our Savior will be attractive to all.

Flee those desires that prevent you from taking on the new nature in Christ! Pursue Godliness and right-eousness, peace, faith and love...and have a wonderful day in His grace!

For Ourselves and All Others As Well

Reference Scripture: 2 Peter 1:16-2:21

Peter's teaching in this passage is one that we all should study and understand, whether we are pastors, teachers, servants, or someone who has been offered other spiritual gifts by our Lord. You see, if we are believers then we must understand that we all have been endowed with spiritual gifts by the Lord. Each one of us has. Some of us have been given gifts to edify the church at large. Some of us have been given gifts to edify the local church. Some of us have been given gifts to evangelize unbelievers and bring them into the church. Some of us have been given the gifts of compassion and service to strengthen and encourage individuals weakened by temptation, strife, grief or fear. Some of us have been given the gift of wisdom, some the gift of works of faith, some the gift of a quiet, joyful, exemplary, committed life. This list could go on and on. But the message is clear, God gives the gifts that He gives to those He wills to give them. Afterward, it is up to us to use them to His glory.

Therefore, all Christians must be careful to remain true to the Gospel of Christ and to the gifts of the Spirit of God so that he or she does not become entangled with other outside influences. You see, it is through the words and actions of the mature Christian that the younger and less mature believers find their mentoring for the foundation of their own new lifestyle. Words misspoken, rebuke without agape, actions unbecoming of a believer, and other self-centered actions of older Christians can cause the younger ones to stumble in their new-found faith. This can bring the Way of Truth into disrepute. What results then? The young believer is not encouraged to grow in his walk. Instead, he is shown that there is no real need to grow. He is not encouraged by witnessing sincere actions of the faithful to seek a closer walk with the God of Truth. In fact, he will likely become disheartened by hypocrisy. How sad it truly is when a believer in Christ fails to honor Him through the faithful practice of the spiritual gifts of the Lord.

OK, I can already hear the often-used excuse that we are all still human and at some point or other will fail to use the gifts that God has given us. Of course that's true! None of us are perfect. Still, that should never be the pretext used as an excuse before even attempting to live rightly. There is a great and obvious difference between hypocrisy and incidental, unintentional weakness. The deceptive actions of hypocrisy repulse almost everyone. Yet, the embarrassing setbacks of human weakness and the corresponding repentance of those who honestly try to walk faithfully will only highlight the impact of God's grace on our lives. For when we fail, we humbly seek His grace much more and determine to grow stronger in that area so as not to fail again. If those around us can see that we are truly and humbly living as faithful Christians by walking in God's agape love, grace and humility then our failings will likely be counted as minor and forgivable events by those who might witness them. It is so true that in our weakness God's strength is shown to be powerful and strong. But it is in witnessing our submission to His strength—not vainly relying upon our own—that others are made stronger. And that is the real purpose of the gifts of the Spirit.

Let it be our goal to never bring the Way of Truth—or our Lord Himself—into disrepute among those around us.

Have a wonderful day in His grace!

Given a Divine Purpose!

Reference Scripture: Ephesians 2:1-10

Even when our spirits were dead from living to please our own sinful natures, God coordinated and enacted His plan to bring us to life through Christ. He planned and accomplished it. We only need to exercise our faith to accept and receive the 'surpassing riches of His grace'. Paul offered a very short retelling of the Gospel message in his letter to the Ephesian church, just to remind them of who they were. But, I think that Paul had a greater point to bring out to these people. And it is a message that clearly speaks to us as well.

His point is evident that it was a work of God's grace by which we have been saved. We did nothing to warrant it. We did nothing to encourage it. We did nothing to deserve it. It was not offered only to those who had a particular merit or qualification. God offered His grace to all who would simply reach up and accept it in faith. Therefore, no one should boast that they have received it. Indeed, if there is a boast to be offered, let the boast be God's, that He has proven Himself to have the power over life and death, over time and space, and the power of creation itself.

No, we have no boast to make at all; except for this…We are simply God's workmanship! He knit us together while we were still in our mother's wombs. He fashioned us and He will, if we only let Him, will mold us into His holy and blameless children. We are His workmanship! We can never claim to be self-made. Can a clay pot turn to the potter and ask why was I made? Can it turn to its maker and say, "You made me as a jar, but I am really a table." No, certainly not. God created us in Christ Jesus for a specific task. That task is to walk in God's ways, namely the practice of His perfect and complete agape love to bring honor to the name of the One, True, and Holy God.

It is not the practice of walking in His ways that will result in receiving grace from God. Contrarily, it is the receiving of Grace that enables us to walk in His ways. First comes the gift of grace and then comes the response on our part. There is no amount of good works that will ever win God's favor (neither is there an action that can remove His love from us!). Practicing benevolence toward our fellow man is a noble task, worthy of respect and encouragement...and it is right to acknowledge this. However, no amount of good deeds will ever sway God to grant His eternal reward to anyone simply based upon those works. Yet, those deeds will naturally result from a thankful heart that has been changed through the love of Christ!

So ponder this today...You are His handiwork. Yes, the same can be said for the moon and the stars, the protozoa and the forests, the lion and the whale. Yet, there is a difference between those things and you. They, simply by their existence, inherently praise and honor God. You, however, have been given a divine purpose! You have been ordained to willfully bring Him praise and honor and glory!

Live in that purpose today and bring honor to the King of glory! And have a wonderful day in His grace!

Great and Precious Promises

Reference Scripture: 2 Peter 1:2-11

This is a wonderful passage, worthy of study, and full of wonderful truths for our life of faith. First it is a good thing to be reminded that every single thing we need for our lives and our godliness has been given to us already! The Gospel declares it! For the simple payment of our practiced belief in Christ we are offered an eternal life of joy as sons and daughters of the one holy God! No other payment will ever be accepted. No amount of good works will reserve this heavenly life for us and no amount of personal sacrifice, compassionate feelings, or good intentions will either. Our active belief in the Gospel of the Son of God, Christ Jesus, is the only thing will justify us before God and open the gates of heaven.

Then, look at what Peter said next. He went on to say that, through God's glory and excellence, He has granted us precious and very great promises, through which we can escape the corruption of our lustful flesh—that is, our whole sinful nature—and then to take on a godlike nature. Why is that lustful nature so corrosive? It is, as Adam Clarke's commentary says, an "irregular, unreasonable, inordinate, and impure desire; desire to have, to do, and to be, what God has prohibited, and what would be ruinous and destructive to us were the desire to be granted. (From Adam Clarke's Commentary, Electronic Database. Copyright (c) 1996 by Biblesoft) In short, lust is a desire to follow after everything selfish and carnal and against the agape (unconditional, sacrificial love) of God. Should this lust gain mastery over us we would never be able to follow Christ's command to agape one another, for we would always seek our own personal pleasure instead of the good of others or the will of God. On the contrary, being free from this slavery to the selfish and lustful nature of sin we will take on God's nature of agape love and always seek to honor others as better than ourselves, as Christ commanded us to.

So, what are those promises that Peter mentioned? What promises could restore our nature? What promises could strengthen us in our struggles against our flesh? Redemption in and through the blood of Jesus, shed on the cross. That's one. The continuing indwelling and influence of the Holy Spirit in our hearts. That's another. The adoption as the sons and daughters of God; the promise of the resurrection; the promise of eternal joy and rest with God in heaven. These are a few of His promises that will empower and sustain us if we believe and trust in them! Through faith in these precious promises of God we can take on a godlike nature and eagerly await, as Paul said, our Savior from heaven, who will one day transform not only our natures, but also our lowly human bodies into glorious and heavenly ones as well! (See Philippians 3:20, 21)

Have a wonderful day zealous for His grace!

He Is the King of Glory

Reference Scripture: Psalm 24

Who is the King of Glory? YAHWEH! Jehovah! Almighty God! He created the universe. He created the earth. He created the whale. He created the bird. He created the atom. If it is He created it! There is no one greater than our God. There is no one more powerful. There is no one more full of grace. There is no one who is His equal in any way!

So what does that mean? What good does it do to list these things out? It reminds that our God governs us and we must serve Him well and honor Him with our heart, mind, body, and soul. Would you serve your employer well, knowing that not doing so would mean termination? Of course. Would you show respect and dedication if you were brought into the office of your supervisor? Yes. Would you give honor to an earthly mayor or governor should you meet him? Certainly! Then know that every day you serve the greatest Employer and come before Him to receive your charge. Every day you are offered the opportunity to meet with One who is greater than any mayor, governor, President or other political leader! He is the ultimate One who deserves ultimate respect. After all, He is the Supreme Regent of the Universe!

Yes, He is the King of Glory. He is our King of Glory! And He bids us to come into His presence! He calls us into His family. He has justified us by His own grace and He has accepted us through the atoning work of Jesus the Christ! So come into His presence and see His majesty! Draw near to Him and He will draw near to you!

Serve Him well today, and have a wonderful day in His grace!

32

Heart on Things Above...

Reference Scripture: Colossians 3:1-17

Here is an interesting though for today: Set your heart on things above.

Where should our hearts be? Should they be mired in the daily toils of making a living? Should they be focused on building a great earthly palace? Should they be absorbed with our clothing, our automobiles, our electronic gadgets, the Internet or other temporary things of the world? No. Our hearts should be set on greater things than these. Our hearts need to be focused on things of great and noble worth, on things that have eternal value and significance to our lives and the lives of those around us.

Our thoughts really should turn to the Lord and to His marvelous deeds on our behalf on a daily basis. Our hearts indeed ought to be grateful that He removed the barriers that once separated us from Him. In doing so He offered us the opportunity to not only enter into his presence, but also to become a part of His family. Our heartfelt meditations should be that God create in us clean hearts to do His work, that we maintain the joy that resulted from the salvation of our souls, that we have steadfast spirits to continue living in faith, and that we have willing spirits to walk in His ways. That is where our hearts should be— firmly set on honoring our God and King! That is a place that is high above the trivial and vain pursuits of earthly life.

There was a missionary named Jim Elliott who once served the Auca Indians in South America. This tribe of people ended up killing him. Most of us know little about him. But we know one thing. His heart was focused on things above. He is quoted as saying, "He is no fool who gives what he cannot keep to gain what he cannot lose." Yes, Mr. Elliott's heart was somewhere far above this earth. With a heart set on things above, he could offer up this life on earth as the first few token steps in the hope of future eternal glory.

Set your hearts on things above today, and have a wonderful day in His grace!

I will sing praise

Reference Scripture: Psalm 104

Once again the psalmist calls out the glory of God. His understanding of the greatness of God was sure. His knowledge of the wonders of God was great. He would continually praise Jehovah for His majesty and awesome strength. From the depths of his soul, the psalmist rejoiced in the Lord and from the core of his being he praised the God of the Ages.

Why not? Who could fail to do so also once he or she fully understands that our God is the God of Creation, the One who set the sun and moon in their places, and the One who breathed life into all living things? Who could fail to honor and praise the King of Kings who offers His lowly subjects every breath of life they take? Who would ever fail to offer the due honor and glory to the King who offers grace, mercy, compassion, and love to His people?

Oh, I have so much to learn! Too often I am that one! I fail to praise Him. I am negligent in honoring Him. The weaknesses of my humanity get in the way and I forget that He alone is God. He alone is worthy of all praise. He *alone* is the Supreme Power in the universe. He is the Giver of my life, the Provider of joy, and the Lover of my soul. Though I am often negligent in honoring Him due to my human nature of sinfulness, in His holy and divine nature of righteousness, God remains forever faithful and still supplies His grace, mercy and love toward me anyway.

Yes, it is true. He is a mighty God that we serve. He is full of wonders and majesty! So wherever we stand—in strength or weakness, in joy or sorrow, health or sickness—let us offer Him our praise today. Let us offer Him our devotion as He already has offered His to us.

May all in the world be filled with His glory today. And may that begin within us!

Have a wonderful day in His grace!

Learning To Do Good Deeds...

Reference Scripture: Titus 3:3-15

Twice in these closing remarks of the letter that Paul wrote to Titus did Paul remind the reader that Christians should 'engage in good deeds'. These 'good' deeds are neither a purchase of nor a prerequisite to our salvation, but instead, they are a natural and genuine response to it. So, instead of the various ways in which we practiced the dishonorable deeds of the flesh prior to coming to know our Lord, we must begin and continue practicing the honorable deeds of the redeemed, renewed life that we have been given.

What are those honorable deeds? Well, for starters, they are the opposite actions to what we practiced beforehand. Take the list at the beginning of this passage and practice the opposite of what is there. We should never practice foolishness or disobedience. Instead, we should live in the wisdom and obedience of God. Nor should we deceive others or become enslaved to lust and pleasures. No, we must live in the self-sacrificial 'agape' love that Jesus commanded us to practice. We should not live in malice, envy or hatred, but should live in kindness and gentleness and hate only the sin that entangles the weak. Anything that belies the kindness and grace of our Savior is dishonorable to His Lordship on our lives and must be put off from our lives.

So then, as Paul said, let us learn to do good. Let us learn to practice the grace of our God toward others around us and as Paul told the church in Rome, "Be devoted to one another in brotherly love. Honor one another above yourselves." (See Romans 12:10 NIV) As a result, the grace of God will be with us...

Have a wonderful day in Him!

Missing the Purpose?

Reference Scripture: James 2:1-13

It is quite obvious that James was talking to Jewish converts to Christianity. These individuals had been taught from their youth to follow the Mosaic Law (that is, the 10 Commandments and associated laws built upon them), so James' statements here were a certainly a tough teaching for them. James was saying to his readers—and to us—that we are not to act as judge toward others by discriminating against them for the way they look or dress, or for any other reason. That goes a long way past simply following religious rules of conduct.

I was once asked what my church would do if a known prostitute walked into our church service and sat down on the front row. I would have liked to say that she would be treated the same way as any other visitor, welcomed, and ministered to. But would I dare? What if an unknown, unmarried teenage girl walked in pregnant? Would she be offered God's grace in its fullness? Would the church help see that her needs were met and introduce her to the God of grace? Would her child be offered the same joy and concern? Or would these individuals be only half-heartedly welcomed by church people who would stand at a distance with practiced smiles and quiet hellos?

Yes, I'd like to say that the body of Christ would embrace those such as these, offering the tender mercy of our loving God and Savior Jesus Christ... But, unfortunately, all too often the body of Christ fails miserably in dealing with those who have deep personal needs. In fact, I'd have to admit that I've missed some opportunities along the way as well...

Still, I have to ask myself, if I am part of the body of Christ, what am I doing to show these individuals that the love of God is greater than time or pen could ever tell, that it goes beyond the highest star and reaches to the lowest hell, and that it reaches even to them in their time of need. There is no discrimination in Christ's love. The homeless, the unwed, the divorced, the wealthy, the poor, the healthy, the sick, the pretty and the not so are all loved by Christ. He died for us all—willingly giving up His own life—because He loved us all that much!

Yes, we are Christ's body. We are His Bride. We are His people. We should be His example to others, or else it must be asked, have we missed His purpose and our calling?

Have a wonderful day in His grace!

Never Fear! Be Faithful!

Reference Scripture: Psalm 107

Somehow when I read this I see a parallel story with what is found in Mark 4, where we read, "A furious squall came up, and the waves broke over the boat, so that it was nearly swamped. Jesus was in the stern, sleeping on a cushion. The disciples woke him and said to him, "Teacher, don't you care if we drown?" To this Jesus got up and commanded the wind and waves, "Quiet! Be still!" And the account goes on to tell us that the wind and waves became calm.

Elsewhere, in Matthew 14 we read that a storm had blown against the boat that the disciples were in. At least 4 of these men were seasoned fisherman who had surely had been in storms before. So, one would think that they would remain calm. Instead, they were afraid! It must have been a big storm to scare these men. Miraculously, Jesus came near the boat, walking on the waves. He told them not to fear because He was God! He said, "Do not fear. I AM!" Then, He summoned Peter to come to Him out on the water.   Strangely, Peter obeyed.   Peter conquered his fear by focusing entirely on Jesus.   But, after stepping out of the boat, he realized where he was. He then became fearful of the wind and waves. And he began to sink. Immediately though, Jesus took hold of Peter, put him back into his boat, and the storm calmed down.

Could Jesus simply have been giving the disciples an object lesson that that they should have already known? Was He trying to tell them that God is the God of creation and that their faith needed to be placed in Him and not in what they could see? Could Jesus simply have been fulfilling the prophecy recorded in Psalm 107 that God would still the storm and waves to calmness? Could Jesus have been backing up His claim of deity by fulfilling the claims of Scripture? Or could Jesus simply have wanted to redeem His chosen from peril?

Yes! Absolutely! Without question, the answer is yes to each and every one of those questions!

Our God is Jehovah, the great Elohim, in whom we should place our deepest and most sincere faith! Even to the point of resting our very lives in His hands we should trust Him. Our God is both a giver and fulfiller of prophecy, for He knows what has gone before and what will come in the future. Therefore, He will never be wrong! On that we can believe and rest our faith. Our God is the God of creation, using the elements around us in both natural and supernatural ways in order to remind us that our faith must rest in His awesome—yet tender—hands. Our God has proved that He is supreme by the acts of His power and might as well as by His compassion and concern for our very lives. Our God deserves our thanks for His unfailing love and His wonderful deeds toward men.

Let us exalt Him, both in our assemblies at church and in our own private times. Let us offer Him the praise He deserves. Let us offer Him our complete trust and devotion. After all, He has already proven Himself to be faithful.

Have a wonderful day in His grace!

Nevertheless, Not My Will

Reference Scripture: Philippians 2:5-16

Is it time for an attitude check? The honest answer should be yes. It should always be time for one. We always ought to double check to see if our attitude resembles Christ's. It is a need to recall 1 Corinthians 6:19-20 where we are told that we are not our own; we were bought at a price and therefore we ought to honor God! How could we honor God except through professed faith in His Son and the humble spirit that faith hones in our lives?

Our mind-set, our opinions, and the exercise of our minds should be the same as the example set by Christ Jesus for us to follow. He was with God, of God, and in fact was God. He did not steal or plunder His nature (the literal meaning of the Greek word translated "grasped"). But instead, He made Himself a nothing. He chose to go from Creator to servant...from glorious to pitiful...from heavenly to earthly...from powerful to weak...from Eternal to mortal...from God to man. In doing so, He held nothing back. He gave His all.

To the humble receiving heart, one question rings out loudly...WHY? Why would He do that? What would cause One so great to become one so small? The answer is breathtakingly simple. He loved us! He wanted to enact the Father's will that no one should perish, but would come to know and glorify the One who is Eternal and experience His eternal life in their own hearts. He came to do the Father's will, not His.

That is the manner of life that we ought to have. Isn't it shameful that we consider Christianity to be just a few church services a week? Isn't it an embarrassment that our Creator gave up His throne, His glory, and His very life while all we sacrifice is a little "sleeping in", a golf game, or a mowing of the yard? No. This should not be! Our attitude should be the same as that of Christ Jesus. If we have confessed Him as our Lord and Savior our priority in life should be singular. We are to honor God by doing His will. Recall what Jesus prayed in the Garden of Gethsemane on the night He was betrayed. He literally begged that if it was possible not to have to go through the crucifixion then let it be. But, NEVERTHELESS, He said He would not follow his own will, but the Father's! That is the attitude we should have…Nevertheless, let the Father's will be done.

My heart is heavy that I lack Christ's attitude far more often than I'd like to. Maybe you would say the same? If so, let's thank Him for His grace that forgave us and granted us His encouragement to try again. Only let us strive to have Christ's attitude from this point forward, for it is Him who will work in us to will and to act according to his good purpose!

Have a wonderful day in His grace!

Our Faith Known Everywhere!

Reference Scripture: 1 Thessalonians 1:2-10

Paul was so excited about the believers in Thessalonica, a city in Greece, because they had accepted the message of Christ and had allowed it to change their lives. Unfortunately though, after they had accepted Jesus they experienced a great amount of suffering as a result. Through this persecution they became a model of Christian behavior, producing works of faith and love with fervor and endurance that stemmed from their hope in Christ. This is the kind of church we remember them as thousands of years later.

Wouldn't it be great if someone said that about us? Wouldn't the world be a better place if we took our faith seriously and lived it out as we should be doing? What would our world be like if all Christians practiced their faith in this way? What strength we would have if there was unity in the body of Christ! What personal strength we would tap into if we were united with our brothers and sisters in Christ! What joy there would be if we all sought to promote Christ above ourselves, soberly thinking of ourselves no higher than we ought and humbly considering others in true respect!

Maybe though, the people in the Thessalonian church had an easier time turning their hearts over to Christ than we do. After all, they were only castigated from their families for turning to Christ. They were only taunted, ridiculed and physically persecuted for their faith. We, on the other hand, have it really hard! We might have to give up certain television shows, movies, sporting events or some social activities. Our sacrifice today is just too difficult to make! These are different times than Bible times and if they had to go through what we do then things surely would be different.

Obviously, I jest with sarcasm here...

The truth is however, that the believers in Thessalonica turned away from the pagan idol worship which had been deeply rooted in their families and society for uncountable years prior. They left all of their past traditions, habits, patterns, religions and even families to serve the one true living God! They turned from their old lives and began walking in the new life found in Jesus. They left the old, dirty rags of worthless religion and put on the pristine clothes of holiness and blamelessness that are found only in a relationship with Almighty God through Jesus Christ!

What is more is that we can do this too! And if we would, future generations may have only good things to say about us, as we have only good things to say about the Thessalonians. In fact, we should hope that future generations look back on us and remember that we practiced those three great gifts of our Savior—faith, hope, and love. The only question that remains is this: Will we live as model believers in Jesus Christ so that our faith can be known everywhere? Really...will we?

Have a wonderful day in His grace!

Our Most Valuable Gift

Reference Scripture: Mark 14:3-9

This story serves a very good purpose for our faith, beyond being a simple memory of an acquaintance of Christ. The meaning reaches beyond the bottle of perfume and even beyond its cost. It even reaches even beyond the shallowness of the others who were present at that time. They were so shallow and indignant that they claimed that some gift to the poor should have been made instead—even though it appears that they were not speaking out of true compassion for the less fortunate.

No, the worth of this story is that Mary gave what she considered very dear and expensive to Jesus. She gave it completely and totally. As a result, Jesus considered the pouring out of this expensive possession on His behalf a beautiful, virtuous act. It reminds me of the statement in Leviticus 27:28 that says, "But nothing that a man owns and devotes to the LORD...may be sold or redeemed; everything so devoted is most holy to the LORD." Often in the Old Testament times, if something was to be devoted to God, it would be totally destroyed and left unusable for any other purpose except to be an intended sacrifice to God.

Isn't that what Mary did for Jesus? She spent some great amount of money to purchase that perfume. Who knows what that sum might have been or when she bought it or what her original purpose was. But, she was moved to break the jar open and devote its contents entirely to Jesus. With the jar broken and all of the contents gone, no other use could be found for them. They were totally spent in devotion to God in the flesh. For that devotion, she has been forever memorialized in Scripture.

Does the spirit of Mary live in us, in our modern times? Does the devotion of this woman live on in our hearts?

Would we take our most valued possessions and give them totally to our God if He walked into our presence? Do we understand that these questions **must** be answered? Our God has come into our presence, and we have come into His! He has redeemed us from our selfish and sinful nature that causes us to live in human pride and materialism. He has called us to be members of His family. He has offered us His Spirit as a counselor and guide to lead us in the ways of truth and remind us of Godly things. He has already done all of these things. And He did it by offering everything He had to us when He—God who became man—died on a Roman cross. Though we deserved none of His love, grace, and mercy, He devoted them to us.

Where, then, is our devotion to Him? May we be mindful that His grace was not given for us to trample beneath our feet. It was given that we might return glory and honor to Him by bowing before the King of Kings and Lord of Lords and offering our most valuable of all gifts—ourselves—totally and entirely to Him.

Have a wonderful day in His grace!

Pleasing in His Sight...

Reference Scripture: Psalm 19

Is it possible to read this psalm and not be moved? I would think that a heart warmed with God's love will surely be touched by the words of King David, the psalmist. He started the psalm with a declaration of the majesty and supremacy of God's power at work in the universe. He wasn't thinking of a simple and specific situation where he was moved at the outcome and thanked a higher power. No, he looked up at the universe and stated that, as a whole in its vastness, complexity, splendor and magnificence, God's creation shouts and proclaims His surpassing greatness and majesty. No one and nothing else besides God gets the glory for creating our world, our solar system, our galaxy, our universe!

Then, David extolled the virtues of YAHWEH's guidance over our lives. He proclaimed that God's ways are perfect, trustworthy, right, radiant, enduring, pure, sure, totally righteous, precious and sweet! Furthermore, following God's ways brings a great reward! God is so great that David could not stop pondering His greatness! God is so powerful and yet so gracious that David could not pull his attention away from the loving care and tender mercies that the Almighty offers!

Still, David knew that he was only a lowly human. He had hidden faults and sins which were transgressions against the perfect nature of this holy God he called out to. He knew that these things would keep him away from the presence of God. So, falling upon the mercy of this great and awesome God, he asked for forgiveness from God and then pleaded to be protected from his habit of leaning on his own selfish human nature by God whose nature is far above his own. That grace and forgiveness is what God offers us still today in Jesus!

Finally, the last words of the psalm speak volumes to me. They represent a heartfelt commitment that his words and motives might be of the kind that would please the Lord. He had just declared how awesome and powerful our God is. He had just exclaimed how perfect and righteous God is. He had then declared that God knows our hidden, inner faults. Now David committed those inner thoughts to God and dedicated them to the only One who could fully know and judge them. There was no casual nature in David's plea here. He was laying his heart bare before a discerning, powerful, awesome God. "May the words of my mouth and the meditation of my heart be pleasing in your sight, O LORD…" What if we were to humbly and sincerely pray this today? How would we be changed?

It is my hope that our hearts *will* be laid so bare before the Almighty today!

Have a wonderful day in His grace!

Real Faith or a Cheap Imitation?

Reference Scripture: 1 Peter 1:22-24

I remember learning something while on a business trip to Las Vegas a couple of years ago. Maybe you already know, but maybe you don't. Las Vegas is all fake! The Eiffel Tower there is a copy. The pyramid is glass not stone. The Forum is not the one in Rome and what looks like marble statues are really plaster. The Venetian canals are inside a mall with a painted cloud ceiling. The volcano is electronic and erupts water, not lava. Even the pirate ship is mechanical. Nothing there, it seems, is original. Everything, it seems, is a copy of something else. Even the entertainment is phony. The entertainers are impressionists, illusionists, painted blue men and fantasy-type characters. Las Vegas is a city that is fake...all the way down to the hopes of the millions of visitors who throw their money away in the many billion-dollar casinos. What is more, the visitors are fake as well. After all, the famous motto is, "What happens in Vegas stays in Vegas." Why? After all, who would want everyone at home to know what kind of person they became while they were there?

And it all made me think! Maybe there is a little bit of Vegas in all of us Christians. On Sunday mornings, we dress nicely, doling out handshakes and smiles and boldly proclaiming that we are doing great, living lives that are perfectly picturesque. We're great. Life is great. We have no worries, no cares, not trials, no weaknesses, no sadness, no pain—nothing at all in our lives that is less than perfect.

YEAH RIGHT! Who are we trying to kid? What are we afraid of? Are we worried that someone else might think our weakness is grounds for ridicule? Maybe it is. But, maybe it is not. Certainly it is not if the ridicule would come from another human who probably has struggled with or is still struggling with the same weakness as we are. Are we afraid of the condemnation of someone else? What hold do they have on our lives or what position above us do they hold that they could oppress us, anyway? Are we afraid of being ostracized for our failings? Who hasn't failed? We all have. We all do. So who would be able to cast that first righteous stone? No one!

None of us are perfect. We all have something that daily reminds us of our humanity and of our need for a Savior! So why do we hide behind the Sunday morning facade of smiles and half-truthful answers to "How are you?" Have we forgotten that we are to bear one another's burdens? Have we ignored the command of our Savior to love one another as Christ loved us (and gave up His throne in heaven to die on a cross to prove it)? Have we forgotten that we are to encourage one another and build one another up, that we are to have sincere love for one another, and that we are to be kind and compassionate, forgiving one another just as Christ forgave us?

Let us, then, put these into action! Let us, then, put our faith to action and share what Christ has given us with those around us! More importantly, though, let us be real to ourselves, our Lord, and others so that we might show the riches of our Savior's grace and love to everyone who sees us! After all, fake is fake. And everyone can spot something that is fake. Right?

Have a wonderful day in His grace!

Remember the Devotion of Your Youth

Reference Scripture: Jeremiah 2

What a message Jeremiah was told to proclaim. Here was a young man, called out by God from before his birth, to be a prophet to the nation of Israel, God's chosen people. He was called out to deliver a very specific message of compassionate, stern chastisement and Godly concern over the sins of Israel. He was one young man called to speak to one large nation that had been torn in two and had experienced defeat at the hands of their enemies. It seemed to him a fearful challenge. "Ah, Sovereign LORD," He said, "I do not know how to speak; I am only a child" (Jeremiah 1:6). His feelings of fear and dread seem apparent, but God's promise to be with him to protect and rescue him gave him the strength to speak out as commanded.

So, looking at what Jeremiah proclaimed in the Lord's strength, do we find why he feared being the messenger? Sure we do. The message he was called to speak through the Spirit was God reprimanding His people for forsaking the Almighty God, Creator of heaven and earth. God's people were worshipping the things they themselves had made instead of Him. Two great sins were being committed by his people. They had turned their backs on the Lord, ignoring His call on their lives, and they had chosen to replace Him with their own imaginations and creations. The message Jeremiah was to proclaim to his people was that it is an evil and bitter thing to forsake God and have no awe of Him. Yeah, I think I can see why he was afraid.

Still, doesn't it seem that many times we fall into the same category as the Israelites? Don't we neglect to think about our God because we're stuck in front of our televisions watching that special series or ball game? Aren't we glued to our computer in that internet networking or game site (or worse...that adult site), or something else just takes all of our time and energy away from our devotional life? Does it not seem that all those good intentions of commitment and devotion we found at church on Sunday seemed to lose their appeal the moment we left the building...that is, if there wasn't something that kept us away from services?

God's message was that it is a terrible thing to forsake Him and have no awe of Him. He is the Creator of the universe! He is God! He is the Almighty! And beyond who He is, He sent Jesus to be the One to bring us into direct conversation with Him. He sent His Son to a worthless, unfaithful and ungrateful people so that He could open up a relationship with them. And that "them" is us...you and me. He granted us an opportunity we could have had in no other way. That opportunity is for us to have direct access to His presence in His throne room. How is it that we could forget what He has done for us and neglect to be fully and continually mindful and devoted to grow in that relationship? The Spring of Living Water wants to overflow our lives with that eternal refreshment, yet we say, "No, not right now, I really rather spend my time in this meaningless activity. Let me get back to you later."

May we grow in His grace, that we might grow ever closer to our Savior! May we truly come to realize how much God really desires us to offer Him our hearts, minds, bodies, and souls. No, that's not being greedy. He's already offered all of His to us. He simply wants us to respond to Him in the same way.

Have a wonderful day in His grace!

Secret Righteousness

Reference Scripture: Matthew 6:1-4

Jesus' teaching here is obvious. Right? We are to be careful not to do our righteous deeds before men so that they can see us being good. And we are to be careful that when we give to someone in need that we don't point to ourselves and announce what we have done, so that we might impress someone by what we have done. The lesson is really quite simple here, but a look a little closer and the meaning widens.

The Greek text uses three words that I'd like to look at this morning. The first is 'dikaiosune' (say it like dik-ah-yos-oo'-nay) and the second is 'eleemosune' (say it like el-eh-ay-mos-oo'-nay). Dikaiosune is the word usually translated as 'righteousness'. In fact, 'dikaiosune' is translated not as the actions of righteousness, but as the *character* of righteousness 92 times in the King James Version New Testament. 'Eleemosune' is a word likewise that means the character of *compassionateness*, i.e. the nature of compassion. Again, this is different from the actions of a compassionate person and points to the nature of the person. And finally, 'apodidomi' (say it like ap-od-eed'-o-mee) is the word from which 'reward' is translated. It means literally 'to give away' or 'to reveal'. The 'reward' spoken of in our English is not a gift as much as it is the revealing by God when He judges the secrets of men's hearts.

So, if we literally interpret the words, we see that the meaning of the lesson goes a bit further than the simple act of performing of some deeds in front of others. It means more fully that the internal intent or motivation of those actions are not to be falsely—or just selfishly—flaunted before them. Our 'righteousness' and our 'compassionateness' are our heart's responses to Christ's sacrifice on our behalf. We are never to 'perform' our 'righteousness' and our 'compassionateness' as a show to others who might be watching. Our righteousness and compassionateness are never supported if we seek man's indebtedness, approval and accolades. Our righteousness and compassionateness are never honored if they are "performed" as selfish actions to gain any return, attention and notoriety.

As redeemed children of God, we are to bring honor and glory to Him, never to ourselves! We are to deny ourselves daily and take up our cross. We are to consider ourselves as living sacrifices, wholly and acceptable to God. We are to lift Him up, not ourselves. Instead, in every way possible we are to make the teaching of our Lord attractive to men, as Paul told Titus. Our selfishness, however thinly veiled, will always be repulsive to men. Our selfishness is the polar opposite of the calling on our lives to be holy and set apart for God's service. Our selfishness will never fulfill Christ's command to love as He loved.

So then, we ought to be righteous, be compassionate, and pray. By Jesus' own words. But we ought to do these things quietly and discretely, when people are not watching and where no one can see us, so that we bring honor to God, for He will 'give us away', rewarding us with rewards that only He can offer. He knows us and He knows our hearts. Let Him be the one who 'gives us away', not our own self-carried spotlights… In this way, He is the One who is honored, not us.

I'll leave that thought for you this morning. I hope it blesses and challenges your heart! It does mine.

Have a wonderful day in His grace!

The Faithful Heart's Desire

Reference Scripture: 2 Chronicles 1:6-12

Would this humble prayer be our prayer if we were made king over God's children? Would it be our prayer if we were made king over anyone? What if we were made supervisor over anyone or if we were even just acknowledged for our efforts and given promotions, awards and accolades? Would our prayer be for God's guidance and wisdom in these situations? Or would our prayer simply be, "Thanks God for blessing me. I'll do my best with what you have given me?"

All too often, I believe we look at faith as a matter of results. If we believe in God things will go better. If we trust in Him things will go our way. If we call on Him He will save us. If we... If I... But is that what faith really is? Faith is not a simple statement of token acknowledgment and a hope of reward. Faith is a heart-felt belief that God is who He promised to be. Solomon looked at a nearly impossible task of governing a great nation and said, "I can't do it. But God, you can..." Solomon didn't say, "I'll do my best and hope you help me, God."

You see, faith is just—and only—our belief in God. It is proven true by how we respond to that belief. It was Solomon living in submission to His God. That is the faith that pleases God. It is the belief that makes us say, "Because I know that God exists and that I am powerless in myself to affect the situation, I submit myself to His plan and guidance." That's the point at which the Lordship of Christ in our lives becomes real. That's the point at which that statement of acknowledgment becomes rubber-meeting-the-road action. That's the point at which miracles happen!

Bear in mind that not everyone who surrenders to the Lord will be offered what Solomon was. Wealth and riches are not promised for us in this lifetime. Fortune and fame are not promised for us either. Let no one tell you otherwise. But the guarantee of the divine guidance of our living Heavenly Father and the presence of His Holy Spirit in our lives is! Our submission to His will for our lives is the great step of faith that is essential for us to fully comprehend just how great and awesome He truly is! Once we take that step, each step following becomes easier.

So how does one submit to His will? Do we have to know everything in advance of our first move? No! That is clearly seen in Solomon's prayer. He did not know what was coming next. He simply prayed for wisdom and knowledge for the journey. Step one is simply to decide that your belief in Him is more than mere token acknowledgment. Step two then, is ask Him to be your guide and the giver of wisdom and knowledge. In other words, if you say that you believe He is your Lord, then become His loyal subject! Listen to His guidance rather than the guidance of the world. Follow His example rather than the examples of worldly people. Honor Him in all you say and do, not just in your Sunday morning church greetings and in your good intentions. And then, three, do His work! After all, you are God's workmanship, created in Christ Jesus to do good works, which God prepared in advance for you to do! (Ephesians 2:10)

So...what is our prayer today?

Have a wonderful day in His grace!

The Flock and the Shepherd

Reference Scripture: Ezekiel 34:17-31

It seems that God was not only upset with the "shepherds" of His people, the leaders of Israel, but also His "flock" as well. The shepherds were out for selfish gain and in their selfishness they deprived the flock. In the same way the flock followed suit and practiced a great selfishness toward each other, as well. Obviously, then, if God was unhappy with one then He'd be unhappy with the other...

Sure this is an Old Testament teaching by a prophet who spoke to a people not yet endowed with the Holy Spirit, but doesn't it sound quite like the Church-at-large today? Why does it seem that God's flock—the Church—has been led into great green pastures of grace and mercy only to hoard it for themselves as if the pasture were theirs alone and might run dry of its life-giving nutrients. Is not the mission of the Church to bring the rest of the flock into the pasture of God's grace?

The rest of the flock? What? You mean there are other people besides my friends in church that are to receive God's grace?

Yes! Absolutely! You see, there are many who hurt, but have no comfort. The church is to reach out to them. They are the ones who cry out, but find no rest. They are the ones whose lives and families or homes have been broken. They are the ones addicted to alcohol or drugs or to something else they've found to bring them an escape from their troubles. They are the ones who are burdened without help. They are the ones who don't look or dress or act the way we think they should. They are the ones Jesus said He came for. What is more is that all of us at one time were (or maybe even still are) them...

Friends, our goal on this earth is not to fill the pews of a church on Sundays. Our goal should not simply be to attend a church that sings the kind of songs we sing, lets us wear our suits or flip-flops to service, offers the kind of donuts we like, or anything else that's of our selfish interest. No, our goal is to be the church that will bring those we meet into the presence of the Heavenly Father who loved them enough to die for them. It does not matter who they are. It makes no difference what they look like, what they've done—or are doing—Jesus died for them so that He could show them His love. He loves them that much! Even more, He charged us to love them just as much too, that they might see Jesus in us.

Share His grace with someone you meet today. Invite them into the pasture of God's grace. Invite them to bask in the warm SONlight that streams from heaven. Let them be drenched in showers of blessings rather than unsettled by torrents of worry and anguish.

So walk in His love today. Take another's hand in yours as you go. And have a wonderful day in His grace!

The God We Call the LORD

Reference Scripture: Deuteronomy 7:6-9

Our Lord is God! We serve the Almighty, the Creator of heaven and earth! It is easy to say, right? But, if so, why then do so many professed believers not seem to understand who he really is?

There was a time when the Almighty looked out over a vast physical void and said, "Let there be light." Light happened. It split the darkness and chased it away. Then He spoke into being the sky, the earth, sun, moon, and stars, animals on land and in the air and seas. Then He made man. All creation owes its birth and current existence to this God we call the Lord. His name, in His own words, is "I AM WHO I AM" (see Exodus 3:14), meaning that there is no greater force than He and that no other power oversees or overrules His will. He is the Almighty. The buck stops with Him and nowhere else.

Yet, though He is great and awesome. Both in power and in presence, He interacts with His creation on a moment by moment basis. He lovingly cares for and provides for His creation. He works to accomplish His will, while He tenderly and willingly guides His people, like the most gracious father we could ever imagine.

Why then do so many people see Him in a different light? Some see Him as a concept, not reality. Some believe Him to be imaginary. Some find Him to be an excuse. Some would say He exists but say He's far away and unconcerned with us. What a pity that these who would say such things have never met God, yet would say such awful things about Him.

No, our God lives and interacts with His people regularly. It is we who have failed to interact with Him in return. And as such, it is not God who needs to be defined, for He is the foundation of life. It is we, ourselves, who must be defined. We must come to an understanding that God created and controls our world, not us. It is God who grants us our breath, our abilities, our talents, our blessings, and yes, our very lives. We exist for one purpose and one purpose only, which is to bring honor and glory to the One who alone is worthy—God.

Strive to bring Him honor today. And if you find yourselves at a crossroads where your will fails to line up with His, then "Stand at the crossroads and look; ask for the ancient paths, ask where the good way is, and walk in it, and you will find rest for your souls" (Jeremiah 6:16 NIV). Our soul's rest is only found in the One who created it...

Have a wonderful day in His grace!

The Importance of Encouragement

Reference Scripture: Romans 1:7-17

This is the opening of the letter that Paul wrote to the church in Rome before he went there for his trial. The letter became what we call the Book of Romans and it is the most formal of all of Paul's letters, probably because he had not met these people yet. That's why it is striking that Paul says that he longed to see these people that he could them bring a spiritual gift. You and I might, when we meet a new believer in Christ, ask them where they go to church or ask them questions to find out what it is that they believe or to find out if they said the same words as we did when we asked Christ into our hearts. Paul, on the other hand, though he was charged and constrained to communicate the full Gospel of Christ to these believers in the capital city of the Roman empire, longed to be encouraged by witnessing their faith and he hoped to encourage them by testifying to them about his. That was the gift he wished to bring them—encouragement in the faith!

In Acts we read of early teachers like Silas and Judas who were prophets that encouraged and strengthened the believers (see Acts 15:32). Paul would later send Tychicus to Ephesus and Colossae specifically to encourage the believers in those cities (see Ephesians 6:22 and Colossians 4:8). He sent Timothy to Thessalonica to encourage the believers there (1Thessalonians 3:2) and to teach believers in that city to encourage each other (1 Thessalonians 4:18, 5:11 and 14). Paul also taught Titus that spiritual elders of the churches should encourage others with sound teachings of faith and that Titus himself should encourage the believers. (Titus 2:6 and 15). These are just a few references to the importance of encouragement in our faith.

So then, are we encouragers? Do we seek to edify other believers? Are we genuinely interested in the welfare of other Christians to the point that we will lay aside the personal opinions and religious traditions we hold to in order to strengthen younger believers to grow closer to Christ and to grow in their faith? Do we realize that encouraging and edifying others is part of the work of the agape love that Christ commanded us to live in? I think we all agree that these things are good. The question is then, do we—or will we—do them?

Encourage someone today and have a wonderful day encouraged in His grace!

The Practice of Faith

Reference Scripture: 1 Thessalonians 4:1-12

We should live in such a way as to please our God. We should even do it in increasing measure, as Paul wrote here. God has sanctified us. That means He set us apart to accomplish His purposes, not our own. Our purposes are motivated by the selfish desires of our senses. We want the things that please us when we see, touch, taste, or feel them. But, God wants us to practice living in the opposite manner. He wants us—actually, He commanded us—to deny ourselves of selfish interests and instead to offer His agape love to others. Furthermore, He wants us to be meek and productive in our daily lives to bring honor to His Name and respectability to the Christian walk.

This teaching is nothing new to us. We've all heard it before. But, I would dare say that to most American Christians it often gets lost in the "Old Time Religion" files. Somehow we have forgotten, lost, or conveniently ignored that this is a teaching that was taught with the 'authority' of the Lord Jesus and that if we reject it we reject God himself. If we willfully dishonor Him on this earth by ignoring His instructions, would we be so bold to expect any other response when we stand before our Lord besides His voice saying, "Depart from me, I never knew you?" That statement should be one we hope never to hear! And we never will if—and only if—we live in the saving faith in Jesus the Christ.

If it isn't already, let the practice of your faith be your passionate ambition today. And have a wonderful day in His grace!

66

The Rebirth of Wind and Spirit

Reference Scripture: John 3:3-12

It's funny how words can mean different things. Often times they might mean something very specifically, but might also appear to say something else as well. This is one of those times. You see, the Greek word for Spirit is 'pneuma'. But, the Greek word for wind is also 'pneuma'.

Now, the writer of the Gospel passage above used 'pneuma' for both words. It is further clear from other teachings in the prophets of the Old Testament that references to water and spirit were common teachings regarding not only cleansing and rebirth, but also cleansing and repentance. A look at Isaiah 44:2-5 would show this. Here God said, "For I will pour water on the thirsty land, and streams on the dry ground; I will pour out my Spirit on your offspring, then...One will say, 'I belong to the LORD'..." Elsewhere, God spoke through a prophet and said, "I will sprinkle clean water on you, and you will be clean...And I will put my Spirit in you and move you to follow my decrees...and I will be your God" (Ezekiel 36:25-28 NIV). So it is clear that Jesus was referencing both a 'birth' in the Spirit of God and a re-birth into a new nature, in this passage.

But look at the word 'pneuma' in the context of 'wind'. The wind blows and we can watch it move the branches of the trees and feel it touch us. But, we do not question where it came from, why it blew or where it went. We also do not refuse to believe in it because it is invisible to our eye. We accept the fact that it came, fulfilled its purpose and then moved on. So it is with everyone born of the wind according to Jesus. He can be felt and heard, but his origins and destinations are unknown to those who are not of the same wind. His purposes are not his own, they are from the One who moved him to act. His presence will be felt and his actions will be obvious, but his personal input and motivations will never be questioned. There is always a Higher Power behind his actions. The one who is born of the Spirit is motivated and empowered by the Spirit and in the words of Isaiah, "will spring up like grass in a meadow, like poplar trees by flowing streams. One will say, 'I belong to the LORD'...another will write on his hand, 'The LORD's'... (See Isaiah 44:4-5 NIV) And all of his actions will be considered as the workings of the great God in heaven. Then, others will remember that the messenger came and went, leaving only God's Good News. The worker fulfilled the task and left, leaving only the blessings of God behind. The wind blew and God blessed. But no one saw the wind! That's what being born of the Spirit is like.

That's the nature of those who have been born again! They come to fulfill a purpose. Then, once that is done, they move on to complete the next mission God appoints them to. They live for God and His purposes alone, and they live as inhabitants of the Kingdom of God though they walk in the kingdom of men. Their beginning is in God and where they go is after Him...just like the wind.

Walk in God's Spirit today...be His wind today...and have a wonderful day in His grace!

The Yearning Soul

Reference Scripture: Psalm 84

Passion! Isn't that what you feel when your read this Psalm is read? The psalmist's soul yearned! His soul felt as if it was on the verge of fainting with longing. His flesh and his heart felt as if they were screaming out, "Lord, I must have you! I can't bear to live without you!"

How could this man cry out and yearn so strongly for a god who is distant and unapproachable, mythical and inanimate, uncaring and unappeasable? How could this man strive for the relationship with something that wasn't real? The answer is, of course, he could not. He could however cry out and yearn for and strive for a living, loving, caring, approachable, very real God! This is especially true when that it is the pleasure of that God to welcome His people into His presence!

Enter into His presence! Set your heart on a pilgrimage to His heart. Don't settle for a casual acquaintance with Him and risk the response, "Depart from me, I never knew you..." Yearn and strive for His joyful acclamation, "Well done, good and faithful servant, enter into my Joy!"

Passion! Isn't that what our relationship with God is all about? God had a passion to show the world that He loved it? Jesus poured out His passion for the Father's work like the blood that flowed from His wounds. The disciples were passionate about God's love. The Psalmist was passionate about God's provision. Likewise, God desires that you be passionate for Him. Love Him with all your heart, mind, soul and strength. And love others the way Jesus did!

Have a wonderful day in His love!

Trusting in the Almighty

Reference Scripture: Psalm 40:1-10

How many of us wait patiently when we are in difficult situations? We want answers to our needs and we want them now. We want resolution to our problems. But we want the resolution to come today. We want...We need...We expect... Yet, if we wait to see what the Lord has in store we will see there is deliverance, for we are promised that "those who hope [i.e. wait in expectation] in the LORD will renew their strength. They will soar on wings like eagles; they will run and not grow weary, they will walk and not be faint." (Read it in Isaiah 40:31 NIV)

The Psalmist was obviously speaking of a time when he was in great despair. He cried out in anguish as he was feeling lonely and dominated by the horrible pit and sticky mud of life's circumstances. If he could take a step in one direction to help himself, he would. But it was as if his feet were stuck in muddy clay and he was unable free himself. He was helpless and he knew it. So he called out to Jehovah, YAHWEH, the Self-existent, All-powerful, Almighty God. Only God could help his helplessness. Only God could rescue his despairing soul. Only God could turn his cry of despair into songs of joy and praise!

Yes, only the Almighty God has the breath of life to give to the one who asks. Only God has the power of deliverance and restoration that our despairing souls seek. May others who see God's deliverance in our lives be moved to awe and wonder at the strength and compassion of the Almighty! May those understand His might and grace put their trust in Him! He is worthy, for we could never even count His wonders. He placed the stars into the heavens, holds the waters of the oceans in the palms of His hands, yet can count the grains of sand on the beaches and knows the numbers of hairs on our heads. He created the heavens and earth, placing the sun to guide the day and the moon to light the night, yet knew each of us before we took our first breath. He spoke and all creation came into existence. He shouted and Lazarus came out of the tomb, but He whispered tenderly and renewed my heart to follow after Him.

May you and I truly see the awesomeness of Jehovah and learn to put our trust in Him as we live our daily lives. Then we might know—as David the Psalmist knew—that blessed (i.e. *ultimately* happy) is the one who trusts in the Almighty!

Have a wonderful day in His grace!

Yielding and Yearning

Scripture reference: Psalm 63

What passion! What devotion! What love for the Lord! How incredible are the words of this psalm of David who has been called "a man after God's heart."

Look at the words he used. I seek you. I thirst for you. I long for you. Your love is better than life itself! I will sing to you. I am satisfied in you. I will praise you. I cling to you. I am amazed at how he seemed to feel that he could not take a breath if it were not for God's provision. I am challenged by the feeling that David seemed to say, "God, I would waste away if it weren't for you..."

Yet, here is the truth of the matter... He was exactly correct! No breath we take is ours to own. It is a gift of God. Every single one of them is loaned to us through the love and grace of our God! Without His provision and protection we would have nothing, could do nothing, and would be nothing at all. In fact, Acts 17:28 tells us that it is only in Him that we live, move, and exist at all.

So I have to ask myself this question. After all the love that God through Christ has lavished on me, am I willing to lavish mine back on Him? Jehovah in flesh, Jesus Christ, told us that the single greatest commandment is to, "Love the Lord your God with all your heart and with all your soul and with all your mind and with all your strength." (See it in Mark 12:30 NIV)

God, you want me to love you with my whole heart? You want me to love you with my whole mind? You want me to love you with my whole soul and all my strength?

The answer is absolutely and resoundingly yes. The words of our Savior Himself state it plainly. That is the devotion He wants, expects, and deserves. That is the devotion that David offered in Psalm 63. That is the devotion He is asking of me—and you. I cannot find in Scripture any place where He says He will settle for less. In fact, I read in the book of Revelation 3:16 the very opposite. Those who have a halfhearted devotion honestly make Him sick.

So, I'll leave that for you to ponder today. Are you that passionate for God? Am I? I hope so! Oh, I truly hope so...

Have a wonderful day in His grace!

Don't forget to read these devotional
books by Ron Dougherty:

A Christ-Filled Life
A Peace-Filled Life
A Power-Filled Life
A Praise-Filled Life
A Prayer-Filled Life
A Spirit-Filled Life

Be encouraged and challenged

Made in the USA
Monee, IL
07 July 2026

56549099R00046